SPINOSAURUS

by Nick Hunter

Consultant: Mathew J. Wedel, PhD
Western University of Health Sciences
Pomona, California

PEBBLE
a capstone imprint

Published by Pebble, an imprint of Capstone
1710 Roe Crest Drive, North Mankato, Minnesota 56003
capstonepub.com

Copyright © 2026 by Capstone. All rights reserved. No part of this publication may be reproduced in whole or in part, or stored in a retrieval system, or transmitted in any form or by any means, electronic, mechanical, photocopying, recording, or otherwise, without written permission of the publisher.

Library of Congress Cataloging-in-Publication Data is available on the Library of Congress website.

ISBN: 9798875226809 (hardcover)
ISBN: 9798875234194 (paperback)
ISBN: 9798875234200 (ebook PDF)

Summary: Describes Spinosaurus, where it lived, what it ate, how it behaved, how it was discovered, and more.

Editorial Credits
Designer: Dina Her; Media Researcher: Rebekah Hubstenberger; Production Specialist: Tori Abraham

Image Credits
Alamy: imageBROKER.com GmbH & Co. KG/I.Schulz, 5, Phil Wilson/Stocktrek Images, 22; Capstone: Jon Hughes, 4, 7, 8, 9, 13, 14, 18, 24, 25; Getty Images: Arthur Dorety/Stocktrek Images, 21, iStock/Naz-3D, 1, 12, iStock/Vac1, 11, iStock/XiaImages, 20, MARK GARLICK/SCIENCE PHOTO LIBRARY, 19, Mark Stevenson/UIG, 23, Paulo Leite da Silva/Stocktrek Images, 17, ROGER HARRIS/SCIENCE PHOTO LIBRARY, 27; Shutterstock: Ann in the uk, 15 (underwater background), Brendan Howard, 28, ChastityQ, 10, DM7, 15 (spinosaurus), Herschel Hoffmeyer, 16, Kues (background), cover and throughout, Ryan M. Bolton, 26, Warpaint, cover

Any additional websites and resources referenced in this book are not maintained, authorized, or sponsored by Capstone. All product and company names are trademarks™ or registered® trademarks of their respective holders.

Printed and bound in China. 006276

Table of Contents

Giant Spiny Lizard 4
Where in the World? 6
Spinosaurus Bodies 10
What Spinosaurus Ate 16
Life of Spinosaurus 20
Discovering Spinosaurus 26

    Fast Facts 29
    Glossary 30
    Read More 31
    Internet Sites 31
    Index 32
    About the Author 32

Words in **bold** are in the glossary.

Giant Spiny Lizard

What was one of the biggest meat-eating animals ever? Spinosaurus was a real giant!

The bony spines of a Spinosaurus sail

This fierce dinosaur's name means "spiny reptile." It is named after the long spines on its back. These spines make up a large fin or **sail**.

Where in the World?

Spinosaurus lived nearly 100 million years ago. This was during the Cretaceous Period of Earth's history.

Scientists have found **fossils** of Spinosaurus in Egypt and Morocco. These countries are on the north coast of Africa. This area is now hot desert. But Earth was very different when Spinosaurus was alive. This area was wet and marshy. Rivers crossed the land.

Did You Know?

In 2011, dinosaur hunters in Australia found a neck bone from a Spinosaurus. This may show that the dinosaur also lived outside North Africa.

Most dinosaurs lived on land. But Spinosaurus spent lots of time in the water. It lived near the sea. Scientists have also found Spinosaurus fossils near rivers and lakes.

Other dinosaurs also roamed this area. Paralititan was a giant dinosaur that ate plants. Carcharodontosaurus was a deadly meat-eater.

Spinosaurus Bodies

Spinosaurus was up to 18 feet (5.5 meters) tall. It was more than 50 feet (15 m) long. That's as long as six cars in a line. Spinosaurus weighed around 8 tons. It was as heavy as a large tractor.

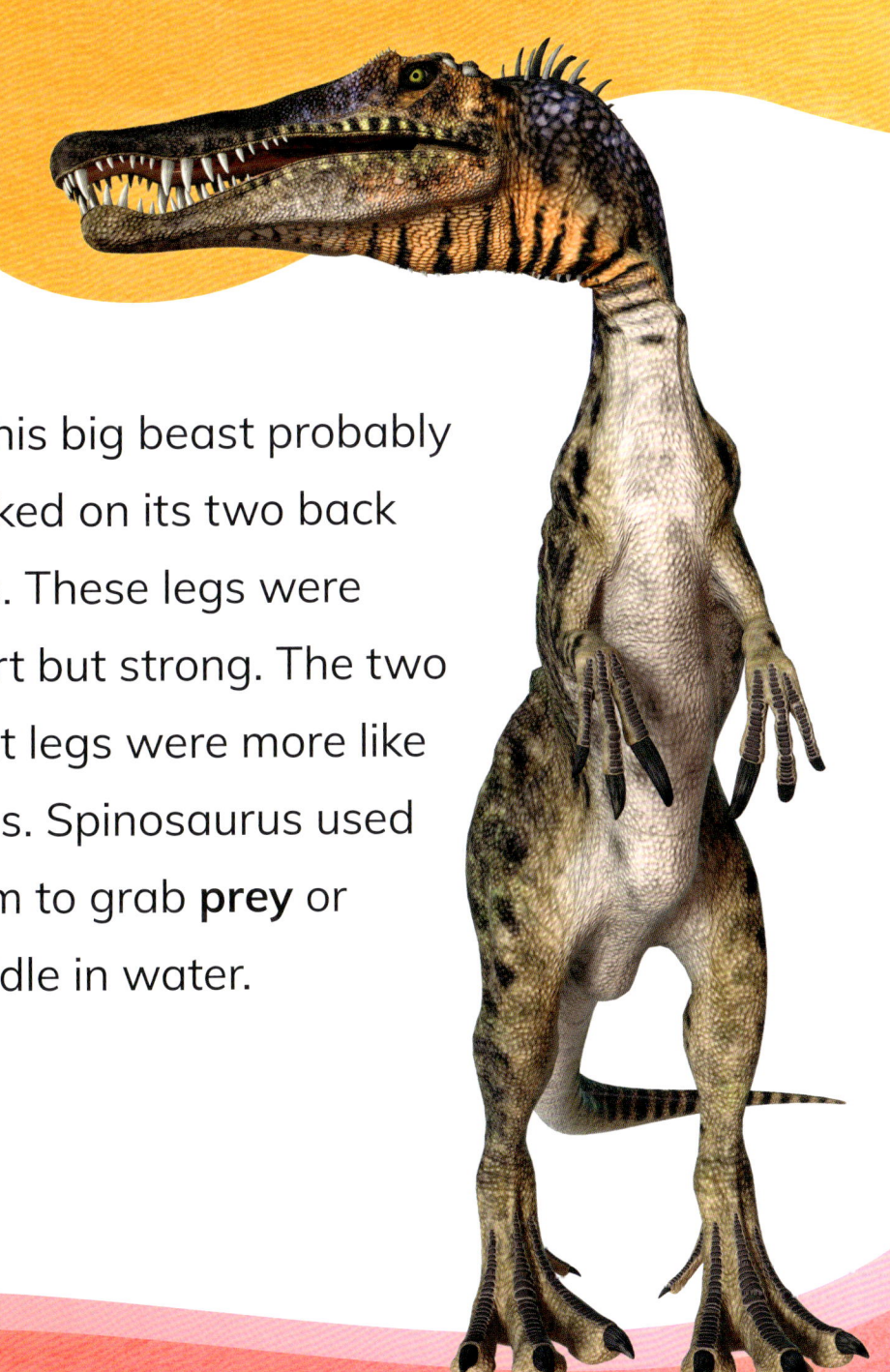

This big beast probably walked on its two back legs. These legs were short but strong. The two front legs were more like arms. Spinosaurus used them to grab **prey** or paddle in water.

The sail on Spinosaurus's back was held up by tall, bony spines. Skin stretched between the spines. Scientists think it could have been brightly colored.

No one is sure why Spinosaurus had a sail. Spinosaurus could have used it to attract a **mate** or warn enemies. The sail could have helped Spinosaurus swim.

Spinosaurus's head was 6 feet (1.8 m) long. That's about as long as an adult human is tall. Its narrow mouth was shaped like a crocodile's mouth. It had rows of sharp teeth.

This dinosaur's body was good for hunting in water. It may have had **webbed** feet for paddling. Webbed feet would help it walk on soft mud. Its wide tail could push it through the water.

What Spinosaurus Ate

Most meat-eating dinosaurs only hunted on land. But Spinosaurus looked for its food in seas and rivers. Its jaws and teeth were shaped for catching huge fish. Its prey included giant sharks and sawfish.

> **Did You Know?**
>
> Spinosaurus's snout may have been able to sense things moving in the water. Crocodiles can also do this. Special parts of the face can feel the smallest ripple.

Spinosaurus had **nostrils** on top of its head. This helped it breathe with most of its head underwater. It could hide in water. Then it could pounce on prey.

Sometimes rivers or lakes went dry. Then Spinosaurus could find food on land. It probably also ate animals that were already dead.

Scientists test fossils to find out what a dinosaur ate. Sometimes they find teeth from one dinosaur stuck in the fossils of another. That's how we know that Spinosaurus ate flying reptiles called Pterosaurs.

A Spinosaurus chases a Pterosaur.

Life of Spinosaurus

Spinosaurus hatched from an egg, like all dinosaurs. A young Spinosaurus may have grown quickly at first. Then it grew more slowly as it got older. Dinosaurs like Spinosaurus could live for around 30 years.

A Carcharodontosaurus hunts an Ouranosaurus.

A young Spinosaurus may have been a target for meat-eaters like Carcharodontosaurus. This **predator** attacked other dinosaurs. It probably moved faster on land than Spinosaurus.

Some scientists think Spinosaurus was a good swimmer and moved best in water. They say the dinosaur's short legs and long body would keep it from moving easily on land.

Other experts think that Spinosaurus did not swim well. It only hunted in shallow water.

Spinosaurus may have lived apart from other dinosaurs. It hunted alone. The tall sail warned other predators to avoid Spinosaurus.

Did You Know?

Spinosaurus was bigger than Tyrannosaurus. These two giant meat-eaters never met. Spinosaurus lived millions of years before Tyrannosaurus.

Discovering Spinosaurus

Everything we know about dinosaurs comes from finding fossils. Fossils can include bones, teeth, or footprints of dinosaurs. Scientists have only found a few fossils of Spinosaurus.

A Spinosaurus tooth fossil

Scientists created this model of what a complete Spinosaurus fossil might look like.

The first fossil of Spinosaurus was found in Egypt in 1912. These fossils were put in a museum. Then the museum was destroyed in a war. No more Spinosaurus fossils were found until the 1990s.

Fossils discovered in Morocco in 2014 changed what we know. They showed that Spinosaurus spent more time in water than other dinosaurs.

No one has found a complete **skeleton** of Spinosaurus. More fossils probably lie hidden in the Sahara desert. Scientists hope to find them. There is much more to learn about Spinosaurus.

Spinosaurus appeared on a Cambodian postage stamp in the 1990s.

Fast Facts

Name: Spinosaurus ("spiny reptile")

Lived: Late Cretaceous Period (99–94 million years ago)

Range: North Africa (Egypt, Morocco)

Habitat: Tropical swamps, rivers, and coasts

Food: Fish and sea creatures; other animals; animal remains

Threats: Carcharodontosaurus

Discovered: Bahariya Oasis, Egypt, 1912

Glossary

fossil (FAH-suhl)—the remains or traces of a living thing from many years ago

mate (MAYT)—a partner to produce offspring with

nostril (NAH-strul)—an outer opening in the nose used for breathing

predator (PRED-uh-tur)—an animal that hunts other animals for food

prey (PRAY)—an animal that is hunted and eaten by another animal

sail (SAYL)—the tall fin on the back of a Spinosaurus, made of skin stretched over long bones

skeleton (SKEL-uh-tun)—the structure of bones that supports the body of an animal

webbed (WEBD)—connected by skin between toes or fingers to help an animal swim

Read More

Clausen-Grace, Nicki. *Spinosaurus*. Mankato, MN: Black Rabbit Books, 2024.

Gregory, Josh. *Discover the Spinosaurus*. Ann Arbor, MI: Cherry Lake Publishing, 2025.

Sabelko, Rebecca. *Spinosaurus*. Minneapolis: Bellwether Media, 2021.

Internet Sites

American Museum of Natural History: Dinosaurs
amnh.org/dinosaurs

Field Museum: Sobek the Spinosaurus
fieldmuseum.org/exhibition/spinosaurus

National Geographic Kids: Spinosaurus
kids.nationalgeographic.com/animals/prehistoric/facts/spinosaurus

Index

bones, 7, 26

discovery, 27, 28, 29

eggs, 20

food, 16, 18, 19, 29

fossils, 6, 8, 19, 26, 27, 28

hunting, 15, 16, 17, 23, 24

legs, 11, 22

name, 5, 29

nostrils, 17

predators, 21, 24, 29

prey, 11, 16, 17, 18, 19, 29

sail, 5, 12, 13, 24

size, 4, 10, 14, 25

spines, 5, 12

swimming, 13, 22, 23

tail, 15

teeth, 14, 16, 19, 26

when it lived, 6, 29

where it lived, 6, 7, 8, 29

About the Author

Nick Hunter has written more than 100 books for young people, including several on dinosaurs and prehistoric life. He is fascinated by the way that scientists learn about dinosaurs by studying fossils. New discoveries are being made all the time. Nick lives in Oxford, United Kingdom, with his wife and two sons.